D1625354

From Love,
koala

A LOVER'S GUIDE TO THE

Kama
Sutra

By Virginia Reynolds

PETER PAUPER PRESS, INC.
WHITE PLAINS, NEW YORK

For HB

Special thanks to Ama Patterson and the
Taconic Writers for their unflagging support

The quotations that appear in this book have been
excerpted from *The Kama Sutra of Vatsyayana*, translated
by Sir Richard Burton and F. F. Arbuthnot in 1883.

Illustrations copyright © 2002
Ann Boyajian/Lilla Rogers Studio

Copyright © 2002
Peter Pauper Press, Inc.
202 Mamaroneck Avenue
White Plains, NY 10601
All rights reserved
ISBN 0-88088-078-3
Printed in China
14   13   12   11

Visit us at www.peterpauper.com

A LOVER'S GUIDE TO THE

Kama
Sutra

SIGHTS

Set the scene. Prepare a special place—bedroom, tent, woodland cabin. Soft lighting, lush textures, and pleasing colors create an atmosphere conducive to relaxation and sensuality. The **Kama Sutra** suggests fresh, fragrant flowers, and clean, luxurious furnishings in a harmonious setting with gardens and other trappings.

SOUNDS

Music is ever the accompaniment of love
and lovemaking. While the **Kama Sutra**
advises the convenient placement of a
lute so that lovers may serenade each
other, you might choose a favorite CD or
allow the sounds of nature to filter
through your open windows. Try to block
out unpleasant noise and distractions.
Speak softly. Read aloud from Ovid,
Anaïs Nin, and other erotic works.

SCENTS

Scented candles, aromatherapy oils, and incense enhance the mood of your love environment. Your scent is your sensual signature. If you place a drop of your special perfume on a handkerchief and slip it into your lover's pocket, he can call up sensual memories with a single breath. Perfumes should be subtle, never overpowering. Anoint your pulse points—

temples, wrists, the backs of your knees—
or ask your lover to do this for you.

FLAVORS

From the sweetness of a peach to the
tingle of spice on the skin, sharing food
can be intimate, playful, and erotic.
Experiment with feeding each other
different tastes and textures. Lick each
other's fingers. But avoid heavy meals,

as they tend to make you lethargic and sleepy.

TOUCHING

The **Kama Sutra** describes a courtship that begins with minimal contact and culminates in the lovers undressing each other, but still refraining from inter-course. Lovers attuned to their partner's moods can arouse each other with the lightest touch—fingertips on the inside of

the wrist, brushing up against the
beloved in a crowded place . . . Each
knows what the other is thinking. These
shared secrets are only a touch away.

"... He should feel the whole
of her body with his hands,
and kiss her all over...."

Ready for Love

_" . . . He should tell her how much
he loves her, and describe to
her the hopes which he . . .
entertained regarding her."_

GROOMING

"The householder . . . should wash his teeth, apply a limited quantity of ointments and perfumes to his body. . . . He should bathe daily, anoint his body with oil . . . and the sweat of the armpits should be removed."

The rules haven't changed much in 1,500 years. Good hygiene is important for body, spirit, and sexuality. Awareness of yourself in a sensual way can open the door to arousal.

Bathing and showering refresh you from head to toe. Bathing with your lover is relaxing, sexy, and delightful. *"He should place his hands upon her thighs and shampoo them . . . he should then shampoo the joints of her thighs."*

Any kind of grooming that you do to yourself can also be done by your partner—manicure, pedicure, hair washing, even shaving, if you are careful. During the time of the **Kama Sutra,** both men and women shaved their body hair.

The **Kama Sutra** advises lovers to

chew betel leaves to freshen their breath.
Lovers today can avail themselves of
toothbrushes and mouthwash.

MASSAGE

Although not specifically mentioned in
the **Kama Sutra,** massage can be both
exciting and deeply relaxing.

Like lovemaking, massage should be
performed in a tranquil setting, with
pleasant lighting and sounds. Keep soft

textures next to your skin while maintaining a comfortable temperature in the room. Let contact be skin-to-skin.

Practice different types of touching. Learn your lover's skin with your eyes closed, using your fingertips. Use different pressures on different body parts—firm kneading for tense shoulders, gentle manipulation for tired feet—and watch your partner's response. Take turns. A light, feathery touch can bring about delicious shivers.

Experiment with scented oils and

lotions; your hands will glide over your lover's body. Hold or rub oil in your hands for a few seconds to warm it and release its aromatic properties.

Try touching your lover with different textures: silk, velvet, a feather, your hair. You'll learn how to please each other with no words spoken.

SAFE SEX

Sex involves trust between lovers. Safe sex prevents pregnancy and disease. It is difficult to trust your partner or ascend the heights of passion if you are worried about either of these. Both partners are responsible for ensuring a safe sexual experience.

New lovers usually don't know each other's sexual history, and should use condoms to protect themselves from sexually transmitted diseases and unplanned pregnancies. With a little skill and practice, condom use can become part of sex play.

Some lovers in committed relationships maintain safe sexual practices indefinitely in order to promote relaxation, trust, and pleasure.

KEGEL EXERCISES

These simple exercises strengthen the PC (pubococcygeal) muscle and can greatly increase a woman's enjoyment during sex by enabling her to practice the tightening techniques described in the "Positions" section. Women can learn the location and "feel" of this muscle as they urinate. Practice stopping the flow mid-stream to learn the basic technique of tightening the muscle. It is easy to practice these exercises any time, repeating a series of tighten-and-release contractions several times a day. You can also gauge the strength of the muscle contractions using your finger. Kegel exercises are especially useful after childbirth, to tone and recondition stretched muscles.

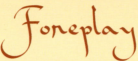

Foreplay

"It is said by some that there

is no fixed time or order

between the embrace

[and] the kiss . . ."

"… All these things should be done generally before sexual union takes place. … Vatsyayana, however, thinks that anything may take place at any time for love does not care for time or order."

KISSING

Kissing is an art form. Kisses may be quick, teasing, luxurious, tender, searching, intense; there is no limit to the emotions that kissing can kindle. A skillful lover uses a variety of kisses both to inflame passion and to prolong the sexual experience. Nuzzling, nibbling, licking, and other mouth play also produce powerful reactions.

The **Kama Sutra** begins by describing simple kisses on the mouth:

The **Straight Kiss** may be the first kiss you share. It is simple and direct lip contact . . . but can lead to much more.

The **Bent Kiss,** where lovers bend and turn their heads to each other, is more intense and passionate. Lovers kissing this way often use their tongues. A classic "movie" kiss, this is the kind of kiss in which you can lose yourself.

Remember when kissing was the biggest thrill in your teenage life? Revisit your school days and play kissing games. Steal kisses; tease with kisses. Stolen passion is sweet and spicy.

"The following are the places for kissing: the forehead, the eyes, the cheeks, the throat, the bosom, the breasts, the lips, and the interior of the mouth."

There is even a name for the kiss you give a photograph: the **Kiss of Intention.**

There are a number of different kisses you can use to make your desire known to your lover.

Nuzzle your lover's shoulder and cheek to gently awaken him. This is called the **Kiss That Kindles Love—** the perfect Sunday morning kiss.

Gone to bed early but not quite asleep? If a man kisses his lover lightly as she drowses, he uses the **Kiss That Awakens.** *"On such an occasion the woman may pretend to be asleep at the time of her lover's arrival, so that she*

*may know his intention and obtain
respect from him."*

If you want to divert someone's
attention from the ball game on TV so
that you can engage in another kind of
contact sport, try the **Kiss That Turns
Away.** Touch him where you'd like to be
touched, and there will be no mistaking
your intentions.

You need not limit yourselves to
mouth kissing. Use the above techniques
all over the body. You can ignite passion
with a row of kisses beginning at your

lover's throat and traveling down the body. Kiss the hollows of your lover's body: the throat, collarbone, small of the back.

Kissing often leads to licking and sucking. While this is pleasurable anywhere on the body, pay special attention to the breasts and nipples. A little experimentation will lead you to secret erogenous zones—the backs of the knees, the instep, the ear lobes.

EMBRACING

*"The embrace . . . indicates
the mutual love of a man and woman
who have come together."*

There can be no lovemaking without
embracing. The embrace flows through
the act of love, before, during, and after,
connecting the lovers in body, mind, and
spirit. There are different embraces for
every stage of lovemaking. *"Even those*

embraces that are not mentioned . . .
should be practiced at the time of sexual
enjoyment, if they are in any way con-
ducive to the increase of love or passion."
Your mutual pleasure will guide you.

Tender embraces include the
Embrace of the Forehead—an affectionate caress of the eyes, forehead, and
face—and the **Embrace of the Breasts.**
This embrace brings the upper bodies of
the lovers into contact, as in a smolder-
ing, slow dance.

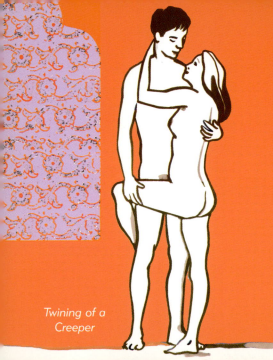

*Twining of a
Creeper*

The embrace to the left illustrates the **Twining of a Creeper.** The woman clings to her lover, wrapping around him, bringing his head down for a kiss.

Another standing embrace is **Climbing a Tree**—accomplished just as it sounds. At the top of the tree is a kiss.

If a woman brushes her breasts against her lover's body as she walks past, this is the **Piercing Embrace.**

If, when lying together, the man presses one of his legs between the woman's thighs—or if she does this to him—it is the **Embrace of the Thighs.**

Women: Imagine lying with your hair

loose and flowing around you, while your lover urgently presses against you. This is the **Embrace of the Jaghana.**

More intimate still . . . The **Mixture of Sesamum Seed with Rice** brings lovers so close that they cannot tell where one ends and the other begins. Every part of the body touches, encircles, entwines.

The **Milk and Water Embrace** can occur any time during lovemaking. The woman sits on her lover's lap with her legs wrapped around him. They wrap their arms around each other, letting togetherness flow . . . they are the only two people in the world.

Milk and Water
Embrace

Oral Pleasure

"In all these things connected with love, everybody should act according to the custom of his country, and his own inclination."

During the time of the **Kama Sutra,**
oral pleasure was believed to be practiced mainly by eunuchs and prostitutes.
Attitudes have changed. The techniques
described for the **Auparishataka,** or
"Mouth Congress," can be a part of all
lovers' repertoires.

Oral pleasure can be an end in itself,
leading to orgasm, or it can be an exciting prelude to intercourse.

FELLATIO

The **Kama Sutra** describes eight types or techniques of fellatio, beginning with

Nominal Congress—the most basic. Using your hand, slowly bring your lover's penis between your lips.

With **Inside and Outside Pressing,** use your lips to kiss and apply pressure to the tip and sides of the penis while moving it

into your mouth. Take your time.

The act of licking and sucking the end of your lover's penis is known as **Sucking a Mango Fruit**. If you use your hands as well, you can control your lover's movements and draw out his pleasure.

If you are sufficiently relaxed and comfortable with your lover, you can take the entire penis into your mouth— **Swallowing It Up**. Again, use your hands to control the rate and depth of thrusting.

CUNNILINGUS

This practice is barely mentioned in the **Kama Sutra,** except to say that women in harems sometimes practiced it on each other. Its definite appeal was noted: *"For the sake of such things, courtesans abandon men of good qualities . . . and become attached to low persons, such as slaves and elephant drivers."*

Although the **Kama Sutra** offers no

poetic names for the techniques of cunnilingus, an updated version might include some of the practices listed below.

Begin with the **Tickling of a Peacock Feather.** Cunnilingus can be explosively pleasurable, although you should start off slowly and gently. The clitoris, the most sensitive part of a woman's body, is as rich with nerve endings as the entire penis.

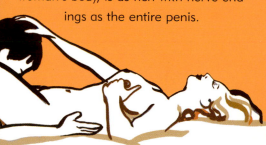

Men, use your fingertips to lightly brush the nest of hair, the crease of the thighs, the belly . . . letting your hand circle slowly around, gradually increasing and focusing pressure. Your partner may wish to guide your hand to the places where she would like to be touched.

As she relaxes under these caresses, move on to the **Trunk of the Elephant.** Allow your fingers and tongue to explore, drawing out every exquisite sensation.

When a man **Worships at the Gate,** he kneels before his lover, parting the labia with his fingertips, before gently

flicking his tongue across the clitoris.
As he worships, he can try different
techniques with his tongue, varying
pressure, speed, and stroke.

*"When a man and woman lie down
in an inverted order, with the head of
the one towards the feet of the other
and carry on this congress, it is
called the 'congress of a crow.'"*

Although the **Congress of a Crow**—
performing simultaneous oral sex on
each other—can be deeply passionate,

some people find it distracting and prefer the excitement of focusing upon the pleasure of each in turn.

THE GENTLE BLOWS OF LOVE

The **Kama Sutra** makes much of biting, scratching, and striking one's lover as part of love play. Biting and scratching were meant to "mark" the beloved as property. While this behavior was ritualized and not intended to cause injury, it is nowadays generally frowned upon. There are times, however, when trusting lovers can mingle pleasure with a little pain, depending upon personal inclination.

"Love bites," created by gentle sucking pressure of the lips and teeth on soft skin—often the neck—advertise your lover's desirability, and mark your recent encounter. A little suction goes a long way. Take care not to break the skin, or cause pain.

"When love becomes intense, pressing with the nails or scratching the body with them is practiced. . ."

Using your nails while clinging to your lover is certainly acceptable; drawing blood is not. Mild scratching can be stimulating, but if your lover complains, be sure to stop at once.

Some lovers incorporate spanking or other light striking into their repertoires. Again, this is a matter of trust and the preferences of the people involved. Only you and your lover can decide how rough love play should become.

"The various modes of enjoyment
are not for all times or for all persons,
but they should only be used at
the proper time, and in the proper
countries and places."

Positions

"About these things there cannot be either enumeration or any definite rule. Congress having once commenced, passion alone gives birth to all the acts of the parties."

The Kama Sutra mentions eight basic positions and their variants, although it frankly states that there are more ways to make love than can ever be listed. Several of the variants require considerable flexibility, especially on the woman's part, and can't be sustained for extended periods, although most people will be able to try them without too much difficulty. There is enough variety to allow lovers every degree of intimacy.

The **Kama Sutra** begins with man-on-top intercourse, usually with the man

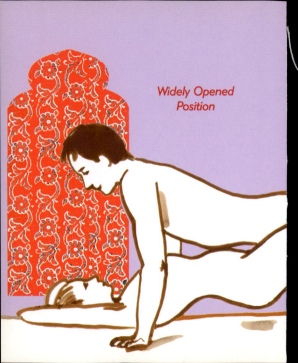

*Widely Opened
Position*

kneeling before his lover. Many of these positions allow for deep penetration and maximum freedom of movement on the part of both partners. The more complex positions described later in this section often begin with these basic postures.

In the **Widely Opened Position**, the woman lies on her back, raising her hips to meet her lover, who thrusts from a kneeling position. The angle of her raised hips ensures deep penetration and

Yawning Position

contact between the base of the penis and the clitoris.

When she raises her parted legs in a "V," this is the **Yawning Position.** Because of the relatively small area of contact between the lovers, they are free to touch genitals, nipples, and other exposed areas. This position also affords a tantalizing view of one another's reactions. If the woman rests her legs on her kneeling lover's shoulders, there will be more contact and deeper penetration. If, with legs raised, she extends first one leg, then, bringing it down, extends the other above his shoulder—scissors fashion—this is called the **Splitting of a Bamboo.** Try it fast; try it slow.

The Yawning Position can lead to the **Rising Position,** wherein the woman squeezes her thighs together and extends her legs vertically, raising them to her lover's shoulder level. The thighs pressing together create friction on the penis and restrict the man's movements, turning him into a veritable "prisoner of love."

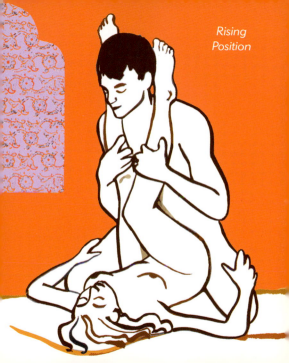

Rising
Position

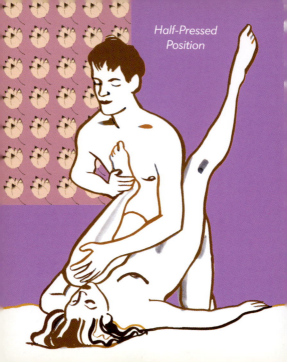

Half-Pressed
Position

To achieve the **Half-Pressed** and **Pressed Positions,** the woman should bring one or both knees close to her chest. Try these in sequence to control the depth of penetration. This position allows her lover to stroke the backs of her knees and thighs, which are in easy reach of his free hands.

Then there's the **Position of the Wife of Indra,** which Indians believed the gods practiced as the highest form of spiritual union. If you wish to imitate the gods, start from the **Pressed Position** (p. 65), with the woman bringing her legs in even closer to her body and pressing her knees into her chest, so that her thighs are almost parallel to the bed—or bower of lotus blossoms. When she presses her feet against her lover's torso, the compact position and restricted movement will tighten the vaginal muscles. Increasing tension in the vagina will heighten pleasure for both partners.

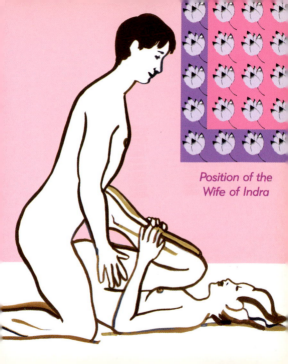

*Position of the
Wife of Indra*

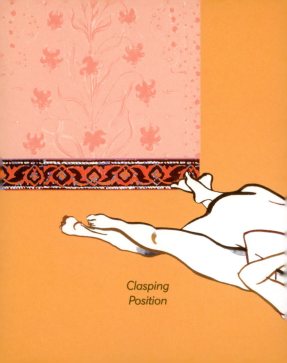

*Clasping
Position*

Several side-by-side and lying down positions allow for close body contact and intimacy.

In the **Clasping Position,** lovers lie intertwined, either alongside each other or with the man on top, bodies touching everywhere. Though not deep, penetration is natural and unhurried. Increased skin contact also allows the lovers to focus on other activities—kissing, or, with free hands, stroking hair, back, and buttocks.

As your ardor deepens, you can move on to the **Pressing Position.** The man raises himself slightly, resting his weight partly on his hands. His lover twines her legs around his and squeezes her thighs to clasp him tightly. Even if penetration is not especially deep, the rhythmic squeezing of her thighs will tighten the vaginal muscles, creating tension and friction. A variant of this position is the **Twining Position**, wherein the woman draws her lover deeply inside her by wrapping one or both legs around his body.

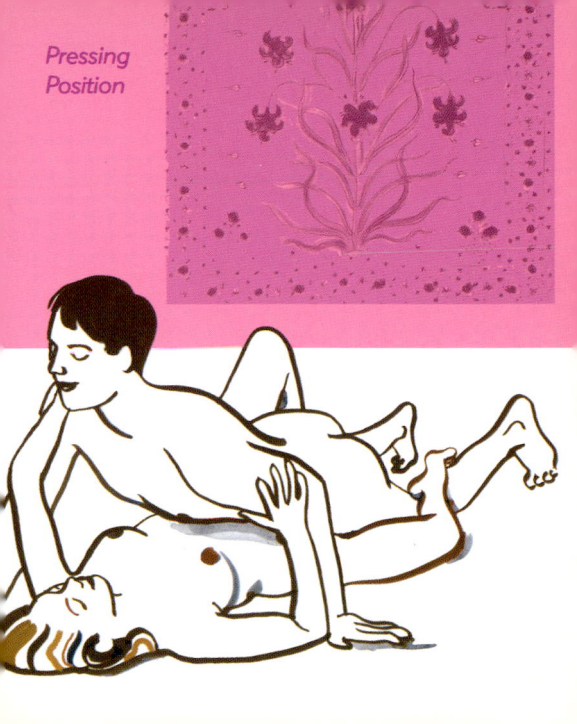

*Pressing
Position*

*Elephant
Posture*

Close contact positions need not be face-to-face. If the lovers lie face down, the man can extend his body along the length of his lover's body and enter her using the **Elephant Posture.** Although penetration is shallow, she can use her knees and thighs to vary the angles. Shallow penetration also allows his penis play around the clitoris and labia—with help from his fingers.

"When a woman sees that her lover is fatigued by constant congress, without having his desire satisfied, she should . . . lay him down upon his back and give him assistance by acting his part. She may also do this to satisfy the curiosity of her lover, or her own desire of novelty."

Although the **Kama Sutra** suggests that women take the active role only occasionally, many find woman-on-top positions satisfying, as they can control the amount and degree of stimulation.

Instead of specific positions for woman-on-top intercourse, the **Kama Sutra** describes techniques enabling women to increase their pleasure and that of their lovers.

If she begins by straddling her lover, a woman can use her vaginal muscles to hold his penis deeply inside. This is known as the **Pair of Tongs.** As she sits straight up, it's easy for either partner to reach the clitoris. Many women find this position an easy road to orgasm.

In the **Swing,** the man sits up or props himself up on his elbows while his lover faces away from him, kneeling astride. This position allows her hands unencumbered access to her clitoris, as well as her partner's thighs and testicles.

She can also pivot her body around, maintaining penetration continuously. The **Kama Sutra** cautions that this position, known as the **Top,** is only learned with much practice.

Swing

More of a technique than a posture, the **Mare's Position** can be employed in almost any of the other positions listed. Women: using the PC muscles, squeeze and release the penis (see Kegel exercise, p. 26). Because it requires concentration, this controlled technique can both delay orgasm and heighten enjoyment for both partners.

The **Kama Sutra** offers detailed descriptions of other techniques and movements employed during intercourse. Some have self-explanatory names, like

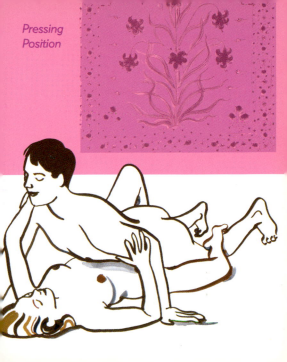

Pressing Position

Elephant Posture

Close contact positions need not be face-to-face. If the lovers lie face down, the man can extend his body along the length of his lover's body and enter her using the **Elephant Posture.** Although penetration is shallow, she can use her knees and thighs to vary the angles. Shallow penetration also allows his penis play around the clitoris and labia—with help from his fingers.

"When a woman sees that her lover is fatigued by constant congress, without having his desire satisfied, she should . . . lay him down upon his back and give him assistance by acting his part. She may also do this to satisfy the curiosity of her lover, or her own desire of novelty."

Although the **Kama Sutra** suggests that women take the active role only occasionally, many find woman-on-top positions satisfying, as they can control the amount and degree of stimulation.

Instead of specific positions for woman-on-top intercourse, the **Kama Sutra** describes techniques enabling women to increase their pleasure and that of their lovers.

If she begins by straddling her lover, a woman can use her vaginal muscles to hold his penis deeply inside. This is known as the **Pair of Tongs.** As she sits straight up, it's easy for either partner to reach the clitoris. Many women find this position an easy road to orgasm.

In the **Swing,** the man sits up or props himself up on his elbows while his lover faces away from him, kneeling astride. This position allows her hands unencumbered access to her clitoris, as well as her partner's thighs and testicles.

She can also pivot her body around, maintaining penetration continuously. The **Kama Sutra** cautions that this position, known as the **Top,** is only learned with much practice.

Swing

More of a technique than a posture, the **Mare's Position** can be employed in almost any of the other positions listed. Women: using the PC muscles, squeeze and release the penis (see Kegel exercise, p. 26). Because it requires concentration, this controlled technique can both delay orgasm and heighten enjoyment for both partners.

The **Kama Sutra** offers detailed descriptions of other techniques and movements employed during intercourse. Some have self-explanatory names, like

Moving Forward, for straightforward penetration; **Churning,** or moving the penis in a circular fashion; and **Pressing**—pressing the penis against the vagina without penetration. Others are more poetic, like the **Blow of a Boar**—rubbing one side of the interior of the vagina with the penis—or the **Sporting of a Sparrow,** for repeated "in-out" motion.

As erotic Indian temple sculptures demonstrate, standing positions allow for great sensual variation. It will be easier—and safer—if you use a wall for support.

In **Suspended Congress,** the man supports his lover under the thighs or buttocks while she embraces his neck. With **Supported Congress,** she keeps one foot on the ground, perhaps leaning back against a wall or pillar. Her lover holds on to her raised thigh as she wraps her free leg around him.

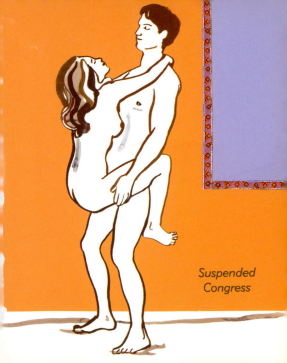

*Suspended
Congress*

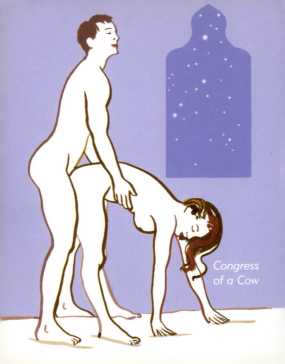

*Congress
of a Cow*

The man can also bend his lover over a table or other surface and initiate intercourse from behind. This is called the **Congress of a Cow.** The **Kama Sutra** encourages lovers to observe and imitate animals in nature, even to name new positions after their observations and practices.

Finally, some of the more complicated acrobatic positions can be enjoyed for variety, experimentation, or just for fun...

Fixing of a Nail

The **Fixing of a Nail** begins with the **Splitting of a Bamboo** (pp. 61-62). Instead of resting her leg on her lover's shoulder, she places her heel on his forehead, and extends her other leg on the bed. His head is the hammer; her leg is the nail. In this position, while supporting his weight with one hand, he can use the other to move or press her leg, creating a variety of sensations.

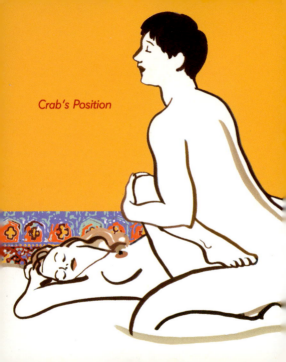

Crab's Position

With the **Crab's Position,** the woman lies on her back and draws up her knees. Her lover thrusts from a kneeling position—much like the **Pressed Position** (p. 65), but more compact. Not only does this position relieve strain on a woman's lower back, it also causes the vagina to tighten around her lover's penis, holding him fast.

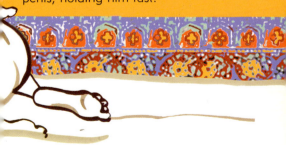

Yoga adepts may want to try the **Lotus-like Position.** As the woman lies on her back, she folds her legs into a cross-legged posture, with her feet resting on her thighs. Her lover is at liberty to take a kneeling approach or to distribute his weight equally on his arms and knees as he lies over her.

Lotus-like Position

Later erotic works from India and elsewhere in Asia list additional positions. When you have exhausted the **Kama Sutra,** you can investigate the delights of **Ananga Ranga** (15th-16th century India), the **Perfumed Garden** (15th century Arabia), or the poetic **pillow books** of medieval Japan.

"A loving pair become blind with passion in the heat of congress and go on with great impetuosity paying not the least regard to excess."

On the subject of orgasm, the **Kama Sutra** falls into coy confusion. *"Males, when engaged in coition, cease of themselves after emission, and are satisfied, but it is not so with females."* The **Kama Sutra** details a man's responsibility to

please his partner, and explains how a man can gauge his lover's reaction. *"The signs of the enjoyment and satisfaction of the woman are as follows: her body relaxes, she closes her eyes, she puts aside all bashfulness, and shows increased willingness to unite the two organs as closely together as possible."*

Sex is a process of ebb and flow, punctuated by moments of indescribable intensity. Orgasm need not signal the end of sex—merely a change of tempo. *"At the first time of sexual union the*

passion of the male is intense, and his time is short, but in subsequent unions . . . the reverse is the case. With the female however it is the contrary, for at the first time her passion is weak and then her time long, but on subsequent occasions on the same day, her passion is intense and her time short, until her passion is satisfied."

Afrenglow

"When the woman is tired she should place her forehead on that of her lover, and should thus take rest . . . and when the woman has rested herself the man should turn round and begin the congress again."

The **Kama Sutra** abounds in affectionate gestures and tender rituals. It advises lovers after congress to bathe, take a little refreshment, and continue to enjoy each other's company. *"The lovers may also sit on the terrace of the palace or house, and enjoy the moonlight, and carry on an agreeable conversation. At this time, too, while the woman lies in his lap... the citizen should show her the different planets, the morning star, the polar star, and the seven Rishis, or Great Bear."*

Whether stargazing or cuddling, sharing quiet moments after sex deepens closeness and strengthens the lovers' union.

Lovemaking underscores the complex harmony of intimate relationships. Using the techniques of the **Kama Sutra,** lovers can compose their own music… so that pleasures may be experienced to the fullest:

"Thus if men and women act according to each other's liking, their love for each other will not be lessened even in one hundred years."